ANIMALS UNDER THREAT

GIANT PANDA

IN DANGER OF EXTINCTION!

Anna Claybourne

Heinemann Library
Chicago, Illinois

© 2005 Heinemann Library
a division of Reed Elsevier Inc.
Chicago, Illinois

Customer Service 888–454–2279

Visit our website at www.heinemannlibrary.com

Photo research by Laura Durman
Designed by Ian Winton and Jo Malivoire
Printed in China by WKT Company Limited

09 08 07 06 05
10 9 8 7 6 5 4 3 2 1

Library of Congress Cataloging-in-Publication Data
Claybourne, Anna.
  Giant panda / Anna Claybourne.
      p. cm. — (Animals under threat)
  Includes bibliographical references and index.
  ISBN 1-4034-5582-1 (hc) — ISBN 1-4034-5689-5 (pbk.)
  1. Giant panda—Juvenile literature. 2. Endangered species—Juvenile literature.
  I. Title. II. Series.
  QL737.C214C59 2004
  599.789—dc22

                              2004000572

Acknowledgments
The author and publisher are grateful to the following for permission to reproduce copyright material: ardea.com p. 8 (Adrian Warren); Corbis pp. 16, 23 (Keren Su), 20 (Dean Conger), 22 (Wolfgang Kaehler), 27 (Pallava Bagla), 32; Corbis Saba p. 36 (David Butow); FLPA pp. 5 (F. Polking), 11 (G. Ellis/Minden Pictures), 37 (M. Newman); Getty Images pp. 29, 38; Getty Images/AFP pp. 13, 15, 31; NHPA pp. 9, 25 (J. Warwick); Okapia/OSF p. 24; OSF pp. 6 (Keren Su), 41 (Dr Derek Bromhall); Panda Trust pp. 17, 39 (Keith & Liz Laidler); Still Pictures p. 21 (Roland Seitre); TeamHusar.com pp. 4, 12, 14, 18, 19, 40 (Lisa & Mike Husar); Uniphoto Press International/Still Pictures p. 26; UNEP/Still Pictures p. 30; © WWF-Canon pp. 28, 33, 35 (Michael Gunther); © WWF-UK pp. 42, 43.

Cover photograph reproduced with permission of G. Ellis/Minden Pictures/FLPA and Corbis.

Every effort has been made to contact copyright holders of any material reproduced in this book. Any omissions will be rectified in subsequent printings if notice is given to the publisher.

Some words are shown in bold, **like this.** You can find out what they mean by looking in the glossary.

Contents

What Is a Giant Panda?

The giant panda is one of the best-known animals in the world. Even though most people have never seen one in person, its appealing shape and black-and-white markings make it instantly recognizable. Unfortunately, pandas are also very rare and could soon die out. There are only about one thousand pandas in the world today. Scientists, governments, and organizations around the world are working hard to save them from **extinction.**

Is it a bear?

The giant panda is a **mammal,** but for a long time scientists have disagreed about exactly which mammal family it belongs to. It looks like a bear, but it is mainly a plant eater. Other bears are hunters. The giant panda is related to the red or lesser panda, which looks like a raccoon, so some experts used to put the panda in the raccoon family.

The panda also shares some features with cats. For example, it has slit-shaped **pupils** in its eyes, and pads on its paws. The Chinese name for the panda, *daxiongmao*, means "large bear-cat." Its scientific name is *Ailuropoda melanoleuca*, which is Latin for "black-and-white cat foot." However, after recent tests on pandas, most scientists agree that pandas belong in the bear family or in a separate, but closely related, group.

This female giant panda is sitting in her mountain forest home in China, clutching a bamboo stem.

The other panda

The red panda, or lesser panda (also known by its Latin name *Ailurus fulgens*), is related to the giant panda, but looks very different. It is much smaller. A giant panda can weigh up to 330 pounds (150 kilograms), but a red panda weighs only around 11 pounds (5 kilograms). The red panda has a long body like a raccoon, and reddish-brown fur. Like giant pandas, red pandas live in mountain forests in China and eat bamboo. They, too, are an **endangered species.**

▲ The red panda is a much smaller relative of the giant panda.

Discovering the panda

Pandas live in remote mountain forests in China. People there have known about giant pandas for thousands of years. In ancient China, panda fur was highly valued for keeping warm. A panda skull has even been found in the grave of an empress who was buried in the second century B.C.E.

Even so, the outside world did not become familiar with pandas until the late 1800s. In 1869, a Frenchman named Père Armand David, saw a giant panda skin while visiting a friend in the Sichuan region of China. On later visits, Père David managed to capture several pandas. He sent their skins and skeletons back to Europe to be studied. In the 1900s, people started to bring live pandas out of China to keep in zoos around the world.

In the 1970s and 1980s, it became widely known that pandas were becoming **endangered,** and they became more and more popular. People flocked to zoos to see panda cubs born in **captivity,** and the panda became the symbol of the World Wildlife Fund (WWF).

Where Do Giant Pandas Live?

The giant panda's natural **habitat** is high up in the mountains of central China, between 3,300 feet (1,000 meters) and 13,000 feet (4,000 meters) above sea level. Here, the slopes are covered with **coniferous** trees and bamboo forests, the panda's favorite food. The temperature is low and the weather can be misty, rainy, or snowy. Pandas like damp surroundings, and usually live near mountain streams, springs, or lakes.

Giant pandas like to live alone, except when they are mating, or when a mother is raising her cubs. Each panda has its own area, or **territory,** where it feeds and sleeps. The steep, rocky, densely forested hillsides allow pandas to hide away and keep to themselves. However, over time, some of the forests have been cut down, and the land has been turned into farms or towns. This has forced pandas to move into remaining areas of forest, giving them less and less space to live in.

At some times of the year, the mountains where pandas live can be cold and snowy. This panda is looking for food in deep snow.

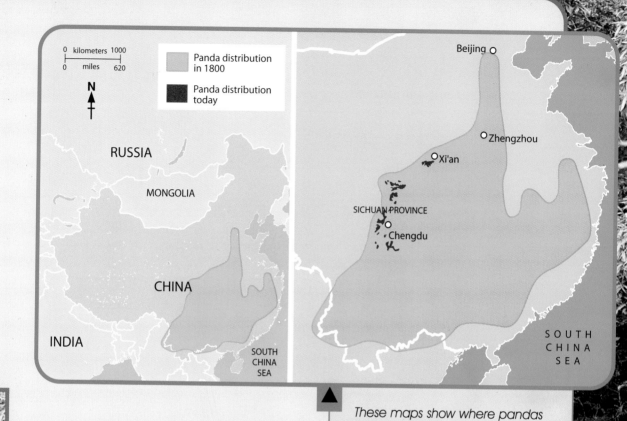

These maps show where pandas used to live 200 years ago and where they live now.

Changing conditions

Today wild pandas only live within a 5,000-square-mile (13,000-square-kilometer) area of forest covering six **isolated** mountain ranges in central China. In the past, their home **range** used to be much bigger. They may have lived across all of southeastern China, and possibly also in neighboring Myanmar (Burma) and Vietnam. It is thought that their range may have shrunk partly because pandas like cool **climates,** and the climate of China may have been cooler than it is now. As the climate warmed up, pandas were able to live only in higher mountain regions.

Separate groups

The panda's natural habitat has also been broken up into many separate areas of mountain forest. Low-lying areas and farms split the wild panda population up into small groups. Known as habitat **fragmentation,** this makes it harder for pandas to move around to find food, or meet a **mate** from another area.

Giant Panda Populations

It is hard to tell exactly how many giant pandas live in the wild. Pandas are very rare. They live alone in wild areas. This makes it difficult for scientists to find and count them. One thing is for certain, there are not many pandas left.

These scientists are tracking a giant panda using footprints left in the snow.

In the mid-1980s, scientists tried to count the panda population. They calculated that there were about one thousand pandas living in the wild. Since that time, the panda's **habitat** has shrunk even more. But a new panda count, held in the years 2000 to 2002, suggests that the panda population has not changed much in the last twenty years. There are probably still around one thousand giant pandas living in China's forests.

Besides those pandas living in the wild, there are also about 140 pandas that live in **captivity**. They live in **reserves**, research stations, and zoos in China and around the world.

Breeding problems

One of the problems facing pandas is that they **breed** very slowly. Even in perfect conditions, with plenty of space and a good choice of males to breed with, a female panda will usually only raise one cub at a time, and might only raise two or three cubs in her lifetime. This means it takes a long time for pandas to build up their numbers.

Habitat **fragmentation** makes it even harder for pandas to breed. Animals need to move around and find **mates** from other areas. If animals mate with members of their own family, their offspring are more likely to have diseases and die young. Animals are healthier if they have a mixture of different **genes** from different communities. Some **isolated** panda populations are made up of as few as twenty individuals, making it hard for each panda to find a suitable mate.

Pandas do not like to breed in captivity. Although scientists and zoos are trying to breed more pandas, the world's tiny panda population is not growing. Unless we can find ways to help pandas breed more, they will continue to be at serious risk of **extinction**.

Six million to one

To get a sense of how few pandas there are in the world, think of it this way: there are 1,000 giant pandas and more than 6 billion human beings in the world. This means that for every 6 million people on Earth, there is just one giant panda.

▶ This mother giant panda at the Wolong Reserve in China is with her young cub. This cub, a male, is just three weeks old.

Giant Pandas Close Up

Traditional tales

An old Chinese folktale gives an explanation for how the panda got its patterns. According to this legend, pandas used to be completely white. A young girl made friends with the pandas and saved a panda cub from being attacked by a leopard. In doing so, she was fatally wounded, and the pandas went to her funeral. Weeping, they put their paws over their eyes and hugged themselves, leaving black marks that they have worn on their fur to this day.

The giant panda does not look like any other animal. Its body is specially **adapted** to its high mountain home, and over time it has developed many unique features.

Mountain weather can be cold and wet. Pandas have adapted to these conditions. While a panda may look soft and cuddly, the outer layer of its fur is very thick and coarse. This fur is covered in an oily, greasy substance produced by its skin. The oil keeps the fur waterproof, which is very important in such a wet **climate.** Underneath this is a layer of shorter, fluffier fur that traps air next to the panda's skin, helping it to keep warm.

Animals and people lose heat from the parts of their bodies that are in contact with the air. A panda's round, bulky body shape helps keep it warm. Compared to its size, very little of the panda's body is in contact with the air, so its body heat does not escape easily.

- Body length 5 to 6 ft (1.5 to 1.8 m)
- Height at shoulder 24 to 31 in. (60 to 80 cm)
- Adult males usually weigh 187 to 275 lb (85 to 125 kg)
- Adult females weigh 157 to 220 lb (70 to 100 kg)

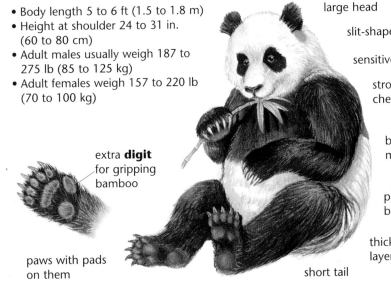

extra **digit** for gripping bamboo

paws with pads on them

large head

slit-shaped pupils

sensitive nose and ears

strong teeth for chewing bamboo

black-and-white markings

plump, rounded body

thick, oily outer layer of fur

short tail

In this picture you can see many of the giant panda's special body features.

In the dark

Pandas are most active at dawn and dusk. Sometimes they also have nocturnal, or nighttime, feeding sessions. Although pandas do not have very good eyesight, their slit-shaped **pupils** can shrink or expand. This way they can let in more light at night, and less during the day. At night, pandas often use their excellent sense of smell to find food. They can also smell when another panda is nearby. Pandas have excellent hearing, too, which helps them detect danger and other pandas.

Panda patterns

Pandas are famous for their black-and-white markings. Although they have few natural enemies, experts think these patterns could have developed to give the panda **camouflage** in its rocky mountain home. The large black shapes help to break up the panda's outline, making it hard to see when it is sitting still against a background of rocks and trees. The black-and-white disguise would have been even more effective in the past, when the panda's **habitat** was colder and more snowy than it is today.

This giant panda is feeding on bamboo. People usually find the panda's large, black eye markings appealing.

Panda eyes

The large spot markings around its eyes help give the panda its attractive appearance, adding to its huge popularity. Humans find large eyes very appealing, because they remind us of young babies. However, pandas are not as cute as they seem. As many scientists have discovered, although pandas are not aggressive, they have sharp claws and can bite very hard if they feel they are in danger.

Food and Feeding

The most important food for giant pandas is bamboo. Pandas do sometimes eat other foods, including flowers, berries, small animals such as mice and pikas (furry mountain **mammals** related to rabbits), and sometimes even fish. However, bamboo normally makes up at least 95 percent of a wild panda's diet.

Large lunch

Bamboo is a tall, thick, tough grass. Because most of a bamboo plant is made up of **fiber,** it contains very little useful **nutrition.** This means that pandas have to eat a large amount of it to be healthy.

Pandas eat most parts of the bamboo plant, including the stalks, leaves, and young shoots. In a typical day, a panda usually eats between 26 and 33 pounds (12 to 15 kilograms) of bamboo. Some pandas have been known to eat up to 44 pounds (20 kilograms) of bamboo in a day. That's at least 10 times as much food as a person eats in a day, even though pandas and humans are a similar size. There are many different **species** of bamboo and pandas will eat several different types, but they prefer arrow bamboo and umbrella bamboo.

When bamboo flowers

Unfortunately, the panda's favorite food plant, bamboo, has an unusual life cycle. Each bamboo plant spends most of its life growing only grassy leaves and stalks. Then, finally, it produces flowers, and later seeds, before dying. After a while, some of the seeds grow into new bamboo plants and the cycle begins again.

A five-month-old panda cub chews some bamboo and plays in the snow after a fresh snowfall.

Most kinds of bamboo live for between 12 and 20 years before flowering and dying, and some have a life cycle of over 50 years. When they do finally flower and die, all of the bamboo plants of the same species flower and die together. This means that a huge area of bamboo, which might be the main source of food for a whole population of pandas, can disappear all at once.

Feeding time at the zoo

Pandas living in **captivity** do not eat as much bamboo as in the wild, because it would be very hard for zookeepers to find all the bamboo they would need. Instead, captive pandas are fed a mixture of other foods, such as rice, carrots, apples, and honey, or on a special bread made of ground bamboo, rice, and corn. The panda food also has **vitamins** added to make sure the pandas stay healthy.

A bamboo diet

Pandas are perfectly **adapted** for eating bamboo. Their front paws have a unique extra **digit** that allows them to grasp a stalk of bamboo firmly. It looks a little like a thumb, but is a part of a panda's wrist bone that has developed into an extra digit. Pandas usually eat sitting up, holding bamboo stalks in their front paws.

Because bamboo is so tough, pandas also have very big molars, or back teeth—five times the size of a human's molars—for grinding up bamboo stalks. Their jaw muscles also have to be very strong to crush the bamboo.

The panda's esophagus (the tube that carries food to the stomach) has a tough lining that scientists think might protect it from bamboo splinters. The panda's stomach also contains strong muscles for mashing and **digesting** the bamboo.

Giant Pandas at Home

Like many wild animals, pandas are **territorial.** This means that each giant panda has its own living space, or territory, which it patrols and guards from other pandas. Having a territory allows each panda to live by itself and find enough food in its own area.

A typical panda territory covers an area of around 1 to 2 .5 square miles (3.5 to 6.5 square kilometers). Pandas mark their territories to show to whom the area belongs. They scratch and chew tree trunks, strip off pieces of bark, and rake the ground with their claws, so other pandas know whose territory it is.

Smelly messages

Pandas also mark their territories with smells. They use urine, droppings, and a unique smelly substance which they make in a special **gland** beneath their tails. By rubbing their backsides on rocks and trees, and using their tails as a brush, they leave this smelly substance all around their territory. Experts think that pandas have such a good sense of smell that they can recognize each other by their scent. Pandas spend a lot of time alone, but they do mingle to some extent, especially males. Male pandas have overlapping **ranges** that they do not defend, so they often wander into the ranges of other pandas. They may spend quite a lot of time in the home ranges of female pandas. Female pandas, on the other hand, do not like to mix with other females. Pandas call to each other using a bleating, yelping noise that some people say sounds like the cry of a human child.

A resting panda uses her extra digit to hold on to a branch above her head.

This young panda is resting on the top of a tree stump at the Wolong Panda Research Center in China.

A place to rest

Except for females giving birth, pandas do not have an actual home, such as a cave or burrow. Instead, each panda spends its time wandering around its territory looking for food, and stopping to eat here and there. Although they can feed at any time of the day or night, pandas often do most of their feeding at dusk, dawn, or nighttime, and sleep for most of the day.

When a panda feels tired, it finds a clump of bamboo, a hollow tree, or an overhanging rock to provide shelter, and lies down to rest. If it has not wandered far, it may use the same **den** two or more nights in a row. Pandas probably have regular dens that they come back to occasionally. Pandas sleep for about 10 hours in every 24, and even when they are not sleeping, they like to rest a lot. They usually move slowly, although they do sometimes roll and tumble down hillsides. Despite their heavy, bulky shape, pandas are also very good at climbing trees, using their sharp claws and the extra **digit** on their front paws to help them grip the branches. They may climb a tree to escape if they feel unsafe, or to take a look at the landscape around them.

Unlike some other types of bears, pandas do not sleep for long periods in the winter, since they can eat bamboo all year round. However, they do move higher up the mountains in summer, when it is too warm for them lower down, and back down in winter when the colder weather comes.

Reproduction

Giant pandas are six years old before they can reproduce. This is longer than most other animals. A female usually raises one cub at a time and takes care of it for up to two years before she is ready to **mate** again. This means that pandas reproduce very slowly, and a panda with a young cub is a rare sight.

There are only a few weeks every spring when a female panda can become pregnant. During this **breeding season,** females give off a special scent and make loud bleating calls to let males know they are ready to mate. Sometimes several different males come to find one female. While she waits in a tree, they may growl at each other, or even fight, until one has managed to chase the others away. Then the male and female play together, rolling around and biting each other gently before mating.

As soon as they have mated, the female runs away, or growls at the male to chase him off her **territory.** The female gives birth and raises her young by herself.

A mother panda feeds her cub as they sit in the snow.

Panda names

Adult male pandas are called boars, and females are known as sows, just like male and female pigs. Young pandas are called cubs, just like bears.

This tiny panda cub is just one day old. It is very small and has not yet grown its black-and-white fur.

Giving birth

A female panda is pregnant for about three to five months. When the mother's cubs are ready to be born, she finds a safe **den,** such as a cave or a hollow tree, and lines it with pieces of bark and bamboo. There she gives birth to one or two tiny, pink cubs. Sometimes there are three cubs, but this is very rare. As soon as a panda cub is born, it starts squeaking and crying. The mother picks it up carefully, using her extra **digit,** and feeds it on milk from her body.

Only room for one

If there is more than one cub, the mother usually only feeds and cares for one of them. The smaller cub starves and dies. Scientists think this may happen because it makes more sense for the mother to concentrate her efforts on caring for one cub, especially if there might be a shortage of food.

Mothers have sometimes been spotted in the wild caring for two cubs, instead of one. This could be because they have adopted the cub of another panda that has died, or it may be a rare case where the mother has decided to raise both cubs.

Tiny cubs

A newborn panda cub is tiny compared to its parents. At birth, it is just 6 inches (15 centimeters) long and weighs around 4 ounces (120 grams), one thousandth of the weight of an adult panda. Newborn cubs have only a fine coating of white hair and no black markings. Their bodies and tails are long and thin. Like puppies and kittens, baby pandas are born with their eyes closed. They do not open them until they are about six weeks old.

Growing Up

Like a human baby, a panda cub is helpless at first. Its mother cradles it constantly, feeding it up to sixteen times a day. When the cub is hungry or wants something, it cries and squeals just as a human baby does.

A week after it is born, the cub starts to develop dark patches around its eyes. By the age of three weeks, it has thick fur with the same black-and-white markings as an adult. After its eyes have opened, at around six weeks old, it starts to crawl, and by three months it can walk easily.

These four-month-old panda twins are rolling and playing together.

Stepping out

At first the mother stays in the **den** with her cub, but when it is about four weeks old she starts to take it out with her when she goes looking for food. She carries the cub in one paw and seems to walk on the knuckles of that paw. She can also hold the cub in her mouth, as most bears do. Cubs start eating bamboo when they are about one year of age. As the cub grows bigger and stronger, it starts to walk on its own and learns to follow its mother. Older panda cubs love to play. They roll around, slide, and tumble down steep slopes and climb on their mothers' backs.

However, the mother still has to keep a close eye on her cub. Although few animals will attack an adult panda, **predators,** such as snow leopards and wild dogs, sometimes hunt and eat young pandas.

Leaving home

By the time it is between eighteen months and two years old a panda cub is nearly the size of an adult. It is ready to leave home. Although it will not be old enough to reproduce until it is about six, it can now survive on its own, leaving its mother to raise new cubs.

Panda life spans

Females can keep giving birth until they are between 12 and 14 years old, so a female could have as many as 5 cubs in her lifetime. However, pandas can live much longer—up to 25 years in the wild. In **captivity,** some pandas have lived to be over 30 years old.

Pandas are usually born in late summer or fall, so a cub reaches the age of eighteen months in early spring. It then moves away from its mother to find its own **territory.** At this age, the young panda may come across other young pandas who are also looking for territories, and spend some time playing with them. Only when they are older will they live completely by themselves.

▲ *These young pandas are one year old, and are big and strong enough to play and chase each other up trees.*

On the Edge of Extinction

In the 1960s the giant panda was listed as rare on the international list of **endangered** and threatened **species.** In 1994 it was classified as endangered. To become officially endangered, a species has to be in danger of **extinction** in all, or a main part, of its natural **range.** Once a species is officially listed as endangered or threatened, it is protected by international laws, such as those against trading in endangered animals' body parts.

Tourists visiting China watch a mother and baby panda playing together at Beijing Zoo.

A critical time

Being endangered is not just about the population of a species falling and falling until there are none left. The number of individual animals of any species needs to stay above a certain number in order for the species to survive. This minimum level of animals is called a critical mass. For most species, the critical mass is at least several hundred animals. Some wildlife experts think that no population of wild animals is safe unless there are about 500 individuals.

Although there are about one thousand giant pandas left, most live in tiny groups, with no more than 150 animals in each **isolated** area. Panda experts think this is one reason why it is so hard for pandas to increase their numbers. Each population is so small that it is very hard for a panda to find a **mate** from a different family. With their current numbers giant pandas are right on the brink of extinction.

People and pandas

Today, people around the world are aware that pandas are endangered. In zoos pandas are among the most popular animals and draw the biggest crowds, especially when they have cubs. For all these reasons, an image of a panda was chosen as the logo, or symbol, of the WWF when it was founded in 1961. People may love pandas, however people are still the main reason panda numbers are falling.

Falling too far

Endangered species can become destined for extinction, even while there are several of them alive. Many species in the world today, such as the baiji, or Chinese river dolphin, are now below their critical mass. This means they will probably die out in the wild. Their only hope is to be bred in **captivity** and released back into the wild at a future date.

The baiji, or Chinese river dolphin, is another endangered species of the region. Unfortunately, the baiji is already doomed to extinction in the wild.

Losing Land

There are two main ways in which people cause problems for giant pandas. The first is **habitat** loss. This happens when people destroy the panda's natural habitat—mountain bamboo forests—to make space for their farms, towns, and roads. When they do not have enough space or a good supply of their natural food, it is hard for pandas to survive.

Many animals need a large amount of space to live in. They have to be able to move around to find food, meet a **mate,** and escape from danger. In the past, large wild animals such as tigers, leopards, and giant pandas were spread out over huge areas, and each individual had plenty of space.

A population explosion

However, in the last few centuries, the human population has exploded, and people have now taken over vast areas of land that used to be wilderness. China has the biggest population of any country in the world, and it increased fastest in the second half of the twentieth century. All of these people needed land to live on and grow food on, so they moved into areas that had previously been uninhabited.

This Chinese mountain village on the edge of th panda's bamboo forest habitat. You can see how the villagers' farmland has taken over so of the hillside.

These workers prepare bamboo to be made into paper.

When people first started to clear mountain forests, they did not always realize how dangerous this would be for pandas and other wild animals. It has only been in the last few decades that we have started to understand how habitat loss affects wild animal **species.**

A useful plant

Besides being the panda's favorite food, bamboo is used in China to make buildings, furniture, paper, and many other things.

Gone forever

Unfortunately, large areas of mountain forest have now been lost. It is very difficult to replace them. On hillsides, trees and plants, such as bamboo, hold soil in place. Once they are cut down, the rain washes some of the soil away, making it hard for those plant species to grow there again. Recreating wild forest areas would also mean moving local people out of the homes and farms they now depend on.

Disappearing bamboo

In China bamboo forests have been disappearing for centuries. In the last few decades they have been cut down faster than ever. As well as being removed to make space for human farms, the forests where pandas live are sometimes chopped down for the **coniferous** wood and bamboo. All this has meant that, since the early 1970s, the area of wild, natural panda habitat has shrunk by more than 50 percent.

Saving Giant Panda Habitats

Over the past few decades, scientists, governments, and wildlife organizations have learned how **habitat** loss affects giant pandas. Now they are working together to try to stop any more panda habitat from disappearing. They are also trying to reverse habitat loss by taking over some developed areas and turning them back into forests. This is one of the most important things people can do to save the giant panda.

The best way to save an area of natural panda habitat is to make it into a **reserve**—a special area where wildlife is protected by law. In a reserve it is illegal to chop down trees or other plants, build houses or farms, or disturb wild animals. China now has more than 30 reserves designed to give giant pandas a safe place to live. In fact, almost all of the pandas that still live in the wild are found in these reserves.

The Wolong Reserve

The biggest and most famous panda reserve is the Wolong (which means "sleepy dragon") Reserve in northwestern Sichuan. It was set up in the 1970s and covers an area of just over 772 square miles (2,000 square kilometers). As well as being home to about 100 wild pandas, it has a research and **breeding** station where scientists can study pandas and breed them in **captivity.**

This photo of part of the Wolong Reserve shows the kind of **habitat** that suits pandas best—steep, mountainous terrain with thick forests and plenty of water.

Alternatives to logging

In 1998 the Chinese government banned commercial **logging** in natural forests in the southwest of the country. Since logging was made illegal, many former logging companies have begun working with the WWF to learn how to use forest resources without harming the environment. The companies have received money from the Chinese government to protect and maintain forests like the ones that they used to cut down.

Some of the old logging companies are now hoping to set up new kinds of businesses that will not harm pandas or their environment. Large numbers of people visiting an area can destroy it. This is especially true when tourists need large hotels, airports, and restaurants. A better approach is to encourage **ecotourism.** Ecotourism means visiting natural habitats in a way that helps to preserve them, not destroy them. China hopes that this kind of tourism will preserve the forests, and help people find work.

A young panda relaxes on a bench at the Wolong Reserve, surrounded by visiting tourists.

In northern Sichuan, the Wanglang Nature Reserve is a protected area that is the home of many **endangered species,** including over 30 giant pandas. Tourist numbers are increasing rapidly from a total of 1,000 tourists in 1997, to 20,000 tourists in 2002. The challenge is to make sure that the large numbers of tourists do not harm the environment and the animals they have come to visit. WWF is now helping to train tour guides to understand how to promote tourism responsibly.

Bamboo corridors

A big problem for pandas is habitat **fragmentation.** Pandas are being divided up into small, **isolated** populations. There are now plans to join some panda groups together by planting long corridors of bamboo to connect different panda areas. The pandas should be able to move between the areas easily, finding food as they go.

Giant Panda Poaching

The second main way people harm giant pandas is by hunting them. Human beings have always regarded pandas as special and even magical. In ancient China, they were highly valued for their fur, because it is very warm and waterproof. It was used to make bedding and cloaks. Wealthy emperors would present their most important guests with panda skins as gifts.

Panda magic

One reason people want to buy panda skins is because of a traditional belief that the skins have magical powers. According to old Chinese folklore, if you sleep on the skin of a giant panda, you will be protected from ghosts, and you will have dreams that will predict your future. Old beliefs like this can be very powerful. Many other animals, such as sea turtles, tigers, and rhinoceroses, have become **endangered** because people believe their body parts have special properties or magical powers. This means people will pay a lot of money for them.

This is part of a giant panda's pelt, or skin. It was found when police arrested a group of smugglers in China in 2001.

This market booth in Myanmar (Burma) is full of animal parts for sale, many from **endangered** species.

More recently, pandas were killed as trophies. Hunters wanted to take home a panda skin, or have a stuffed panda in their house. In the late 1800s and early 1900s, many pandas were also killed by scientists so that they could take panda body parts home to study them or display them in museums.

People have continued to hunt and kill pandas for their skins and as a sport. In the early 1900s, this seriously reduced panda numbers. When there were plenty of pandas, panda numbers could recover more easily. But now, there are so few pandas that killing just one of them makes it more likely that the **species** will die out altogether.

Killing for money

It is now illegal to kill a panda, but people still pay high prices for panda skins on the **black market,** so **poaching** continues today. Despite laws against poaching, there are still a few people in the world who will pay a lot of money for giant panda skins. One skin can fetch several thousand dollars. This is more money than most Chinese farmers can earn in their whole lives. So, it is not surprising that some poor farmers in China still think it is worth the risk to set snares and traps for pandas.

As well as being targeted by poachers, pandas also risk being caught in traps set for other wild animals, such as other types of bears and musk deer.

Stopping Poaching

How can people be stopped from killing giant pandas? One step is to make panda **poaching** illegal and to impose severe punishments on those who break the law. Panda hunting has been illegal in China since the 1960s. Even so, poaching continued out of control. Then, in 1987, the Chinese government made the penalties much stricter. Killing a panda, or smuggling a panda skin, became punishable by a minimum prison sentence of 20 years, or the death sentence. Although judges do not usually impose the death penalty, people can still be sent to jail for life for killing pandas. There are also international laws against trading the skins or other body parts of **endangered species.** So, even outside China, being caught with a panda skin is a serious crime.

This guard is in Wanglang Nature Reserve in Sichuan Province. A panda reserve guard is always on the lookout for pandas, as well as poachers and illegal loggers.

It is hard to get the balance right between strict laws and unreasonable punishments. Many people feel that a death sentence for poaching pandas actually makes it harder to protect them. People will be less likely to turn someone in if that person might be put to death.

Panda visits

Since people have started to take over more areas that used to be occupied by pandas, they have ended up living in closer contact with pandas. There have even been several reports of pandas wandering into villages, farms, and other human settlements. According to one of these stories, in 1983, a giant panda walked into a farmer's home, where it ate a bowl of rice and rested on the bed, before leaving.

Panda police

The problem with laws like this is that they have to be enforced. Although panda **reserves** have rangers who watch out for poachers, it is very difficult to keep watch over wild pandas or catch people who might be trying to poach them. This is because the mountain forest **habitat** is so dense, remote, and hard to travel in. It is also hard to track down panda skins once they have left China. They are not sold in normal stores, but on the **black market,** usually in secret locations.

The first step for panda reserves is to hire more rangers. Rangers also need to be trained. Many rangers are not well paid. They lack equipment, and uniforms, that would help them tackle poachers with confidence. Organizations like the Panda Trust have helped rangers at Wolong, China's biggest giant panda reserve, by providing equipment, such as uniforms, backpacks, video cameras, and radio telephones. The organization has also funded training courses for rangers.

At the BaiShuiHe Nature Reserve in Sichuan, managers plan to build five ranger stations. While the Chinese government is providing funds to build the ranger stations in the reserve, funds are still needed to pay for the rangers.

Poaching has not been stamped out, but it is becoming rarer and is not as much of a problem as it was in the 1980s and 1990s. Making this happen requires constant effort and funds. Strict laws and education programs have to stay in place to keep pandas as safe as possible.

The background in this picture gives an idea of how hard it would be for a ranger to track poachers in such steep and wild terrain.

Helping Local People Help Pandas

Changing the attitudes of local people and businesses is essential if the giant panda is to be saved. As well as making laws, the Chinese government is now working to educate people about the struggles of giant pandas. When they learn that the panda is **endangered,** and that there is a huge international effort to save it, local people are less likely to want to kill one.

Besides setting up **reserves,** the Chinese government is trying to encourage local people to help pandas when they can. It sends teachers to explain to people that pandas are rare and should be protected. Farmers are encouraged to feed hungry pandas who wander onto their land. They are also taught how to grow crops, such as mushrooms, that can grow among the bamboo and forest trees. Many other crops require farmers to cut down trees. Since mushrooms grow among the trees, the panda **habitat** is preserved.

Schoolchildren in China learn about the environment and the importance of saving endangered species.

This farmer is crossing his bamboo fields near the Wolong Panda Research Center. Conservation has to be sensitive to the needs of local people.

Rewarding people

The Chinese government also pays local people to help pandas. The government rewards people, for example, for feeding a panda that is starving, or for protecting a panda that wanders into a village or onto farmland. Although not as high as the price of a dead panda, these cash payments are still high compared to a farmer's normal income. So people have started to regard living pandas as valuable, and will help them when they can.

New approaches

The government is also helping local people in other ways. It has extended electricity cables to some mountain villages, so that villagers can use electric heating instead of chopping down trees for firewood. There are even rescue teams that look for pandas that have run out of bamboo, catch them, and transport them to other areas where there is still plenty of bamboo to eat.

To try to give the pandas back some of their old habitat, people from some farms and towns have even been moved away from the mountain forests. Some fields are being replanted with bamboo. Two different kinds of bamboo are planted in each area, so that if one kind flowers and dies back, the other remains to provide food for pandas. Meanwhile, scientists are developing new fertilizers and plant food that can make bamboo grow faster. This helps recreate panda habitat as quickly as possible.

Thanks to awareness programs and international **conservation** efforts, most Chinese people now see the giant panda as a national treasure and a symbol of China.

It is not just human activity that threatens giant pandas. They are also at risk because they are so **specialized.** Pandas are **adapted** to a very particular **habitat,** lifestyle, and a very specific diet of bamboo. These special needs mean that changes in **climate** or plant life can cause huge problems for pandas.

Bamboo die-offs

One problem with relying on bamboo for a food supply is that, every few years, large areas of bamboo die back and disappear for a while before starting to grow again. When this happens, pandas have to find a new supply of bamboo. In the past, this was not as big of a problem as it is today, because when one area of bamboo died, the pandas could simply move to another area and feed on a different bamboo **species.** Because groups of pandas now live in small, **isolated** areas, cut off from each other by farmland and towns, a bamboo die-off can mean that pandas will starve.

Panda predators

Apart from people, there are not really any **predators** that hunt and kill adult pandas. However, panda cubs are at risk from hunting animals, such as snow leopards and wolves. Again, when pandas were not so rare, this was less of a problem. Some cubs did get eaten, but there were enough young wild cubs that survived. Today each panda community needs every cub in order to keep its population steady.

This snow leopard reveals its sharp meat eater's teeth. Snow leopards are now more likely than ever to kill and eat panda cubs.

Unfortunately, natural predators are more of a risk than ever. One reason is that the predators themselves are in trouble. The snow leopard, for example, is **endangered.** Like the panda, it suffers from habitat loss, and its favorite prey animals, such as wild goats and sheep, are disappearing as farms take over their habitats and food sources. This makes it even more likely that a snow leopard, hungry and searching for any food it can find, will kill and eat a baby panda.

Climate change

While disasters caused by bad weather, such as floods, have killed pandas in the past, future climate change could be even deadlier for pandas. Global warming could also have an impact. If world temperatures continue to rise, animals that are only comfortable in cold climates will be at risk. Higher temperatures could be harmful to pandas as they run out of high altitude forest that remains cool enough for them to live in.

*These villagers are constructing a dike to protect a giant panda **reserve** from floods in the Qin Ling mountains of China's Shaanxi province.*

The 1970s bamboo famine

One of the biggest bamboo flowerings in recent times happened in the late 1970s in the northern part of China's Sichuan province. Sichuan makes up an important part of the giant panda's **range,** and when the bamboo died off, hundreds of pandas were left to starve. This disaster killed many pandas and seriously damaged the panda population. However, it also helped make people aware of the struggle of the panda, and started panda **conservation** efforts around the world. Since the early 1980s the Chinese government has increased its efforts to help pandas. The government has teamed up with international conservation groups to study, monitor, and **breed** pandas.

People have been aware of the giant panda's problems since the Chinese government began to monitor panda populations in the 1950s. However, **conservation** efforts really took off in the 1970s. This is when the Chinese started to build panda research stations and set aside large amounts of land for panda **reserves.**

As the panda's problems became more widely known around the world, conservation organizations from other countries began to work with the Chinese on panda campaigns. The biggest of these was the WWF. This organization works to protect **endangered** wildlife **species** and their **habitats,** through programs such as sending scientists to study endangered animals, raising awareness about endangered species, and running adopt-an-animal programs.

This is the modern version of the famous WWF panda logo.

The panda logo

The panda has been the logo of the WWF for over 40 years. It was based on sketches of Chi Chi, a panda who lived in England at London Zoo in the 1960s. The famous British naturalist Sir Peter Scott, one of the founders of WWF, studied the drawings and designed the famous logo. It has been changed several times to keep it looking modern. Over the years, the logo has helped to make the panda one of the world's most easily recognized animals.

Panda plan

In 1980, the WWF started to work closely with the Chinese government to develop a panda protection plan. Together they have arranged many research trips so that Chinese and foreign scientists can work together to count pandas and learn more about what they need to survive. The WWF also helped to build the world's biggest panda research station and **captive breeding** center at the Wolong Reserve in Sichuan. Today, it continues to campaign for pandas, paying for training for reserve guards and proposing new ideas, such as the bamboo corridor. WWF also helps train local businesses to find ways for local people to make money without damaging pandas and their habitat.

Famous pandas

Now and then pandas have made headline news. Every time this happens it helps remind people about pandas and their struggle. Su Lin was the first panda to be exported alive from China. He was taken to live in a zoo in Chicago, Illinois, in 1936. In 1963 Li-Li became the first panda to give birth in captivity, to Ming-Ming, at Beijing Zoo in China. Chang Chang, the world's oldest panda, died in 2002 at Jinan Zoo in China. He was about 35 years old.

This young WWF volunteer's job is to take visitors on the trail of giant pandas in the Qin Ling mountains of Shaanxi Province, China.

Giant Panda Research

Research means studying something and trying to find out more about it. Several different kinds of scientists carry out research on giant pandas and their lifestyle, **habitat,** behavior, and animal relatives. They include: zoologists, who study animals; ecologists, who study habitats and the wildlife that lives in them; and geneticists, who study the **genes** of living things. Genes are the tiny building blocks of life that make each individual different.

When animals are **endangered,** studying them closely is very important. It helps us to understand what surroundings they need, how they reproduce, and what kinds of food they can survive on. Panda scientists also do research to find out how many pandas there are, and how serious the threat to them is.

Researching pandas, especially in the wild, is hard work. Scientists have to go on long trips, hiking and camping in the forest for several weeks, to follow pandas and find out information about them. China also has special panda research stations where scientists can keep pandas **captive** while they study them.

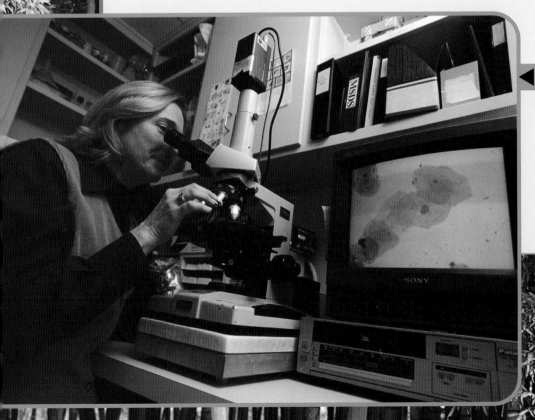

A scientist uses a microscope to study **cells** from a giant panda's body. You can see them on the screen on the right.

Panda clues

A lot of panda research is done without even seeing a panda. Instead, scientists look for tracks and signs that reveal where pandas have been and what they have been doing. Signs include panda footprints, chewed bamboo plants, scratch marks on trees, and panda droppings. Using signs like these, experts can follow a panda's movements and activities. They can also use them to track down and catch a panda for further research.

Radio tracking

To keep tabs on exactly where a panda is, scientists use radio tracking. They catch a panda, using a dart to inject it with a drug that makes it go to sleep for a short time.

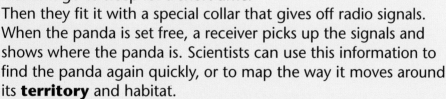

These scientists are radio-tracking a panda. They are holding up antennae to collect radio signals from a radio collar fitted to a giant panda somewhere in the area.

Then they fit it with a special collar that gives off radio signals. When the panda is set free, a receiver picks up the signals and shows where the panda is. Scientists can use this information to find the panda again quickly, or to map the way it moves around its **territory** and habitat.

The Wolong Research Station

China's biggest panda **reserve,** Wolong, also has a scientific research station. There, scientists can keep the pandas they are studying in a safe pen. They also run a **captive breeding** program. Parts of the station are open to the visitors, who come to watch the pandas being fed, and to see mother pandas with their newborn cubs. The station also has science laboratories and living quarters for visiting scientists.

Giant Pandas in Captivity

There are about 140 giant pandas living in zoos and research stations around the world. Most of them are in China, but there are also pandas in Japan, Mexico, Germany, the United Kingdom, and in San Diego, Atlanta, and Washington, D.C. In the past China often rented pandas out to foreign zoos, and used the money to pay for wild panda protection programs. This may be revived to help pay for panda **conservation** in the future.

Through the 1970s and 1980s, pandas became more and more popular with the public. **Captive breeding** programs took off, and whenever a captive panda gave birth it became headline news. People flocked to zoos to see the giant pandas and their cubs. In 1987, when San Diego Zoo borrowed two pandas for a six-month stay, attendance at the zoo increased by a third.

▲ *Students crowd around the pen of Shuan Shuan, a 16-year-old female panda at Tokyo Zoo in Japan.*

Captive breeding

Captive breeding—breeding animals in zoos or breeding stations—is often used to try to increase the numbers of an **endangered species,** and help it to survive. Unfortunately for pandas, they do not breed very well in captivity. It is hard to persuade captive pandas to **mate** at all, and even if a female does manage to give birth, the cubs often die when they are very young. Experts think this may be because giant pandas, especially males, suffer a lot of stress when they are kept in captivity. Pandas naturally prefer to live alone and far away from people. Since panda captive breeding programs began, several hundred pandas have been born in captivity, but less than a quarter of them have survived to adulthood.

These eight panda cubs, four sets of twins, were all born at the Wolong **Reserve** as a result of artificial insemination.

Getting it right

Over the years, however, zoo and panda experts have developed ways to help pandas reproduce in captivity, and to help the cubs survive. One way is to use artificial insemination. This is when **cells** are taken from the male's body and injected into the female's body, so that the pandas do not have to mate. Then, when a female gives birth to two cubs, zoo staff take away the smaller cub, which would normally be left to die, and raise it themselves. This means that both cubs have a chance of surviving. With methods like these, breeders have become much more successful in recent years. Cubs born in the captive breeding program at Wolong, for example, now have almost a 100 percent chance of survival.

A taste for metal

The ancient Chinese studied pandas and their behavior. For example, a geography text from around 500 B.C.E. described them as animals that like to eat metal. Pandas do not really eat metal, but they do like the taste of it. Panda scientists and zoo staff have noticed that after eating their food from metal bowls, pandas often lick and taste the bowls long after the food is all gone. The reason for this is not known, although some people believe that pandas can taste certain elements in the metal that are **nutritionally** important for them.

The Giant Panda's Future

Will the giant panda die out? Experts do not all agree. Some say that along with other very **endangered species,** such as the tiger, the panda could be **extinct** within twenty years. Others think that the panda will probably survive at least throughout the 2000s, and maybe longer.

Although the panda population is small, it has now been stable for about twenty years, and does not seem to be shrinking. Workers at some panda **reserves** in China have reported that they are now seeing more wild pandas than they used to, suggesting that in some areas, pandas finally might be starting to increase their numbers.

This worker at the Wolong Center feeds twin panda cubs on a special kind of milk.

Luckier than some

Pandas are still threatened by **habitat** loss and **poaching,** but they do not suffer from some of the problems that face many other endangered species. For example, they are not usually hunted for their meat, and they are not at risk from the dangerous **viruses** that can harm some other animals. The area where they live is relatively peaceful and not troubled by wars that cause problems for other endangered species, such as gorillas in Africa. On top of all this, the giant panda is at the center of one of the biggest, most expensive, and most famous **conservation** campaigns the world has ever seen. It enjoys massive popularity worldwide, and millions of people around the world support efforts to save it. As long as those efforts continue, the giant panda has a chance of escaping **extinction.**

Scientific solutions

Besides protecting wild pandas and running **captive breeding** programs, conservationists and scientists are working on new methods and inventions to help pandas in the future. Some scientists are working with bamboo to see if they can develop new, faster-growing varieties. **Satellite** technology is also being developed to track pandas in their natural habitat, and to observe areas of wild bamboo to record when they flower and die. In zoos, scientists and zoo staff work on panda **nutrition** to find out what kind of diet gives cubs the best chance of surviving. Before long, scientists may even be able to **clone** pandas.

Dolly the sheep, the first mammal to be successfully cloned, is shown here with her own lamb, Bonnie.

Panda cloning

Cloning means making an animal that is an exact copy of another animal. A cloned animal is made by taking an animal **cell** and inserting its **DNA** into an egg cell from a female. In 1996, scientists in Scotland successfully created a cloned sheep, named Dolly, and since then several other types of **mammals** have been cloned. Conservationists soon realized they might be able to use cloning to increase the numbers of endangered species, and now scientists at the Chinese Academy of Sciences in Beijing have started work on a panda cloning program. They plan to implant the cloned panda cell in the womb of another animal, such as a bear. However, there are still problems with cloning. Cloned animals often die soon after birth, or suffer from diseases later in life. Cloning might one day be able to help the giant panda, but only if these problems are solved.

How Can You Help?

If you want to join in the international effort to save the giant panda, there are lots of things you can do. It is easy to become a member of a **conservation** organization, such as WWF or the Panda Trust. By paying your membership, you can help to fund conservation activities. You might also receive a magazine, a badge, and stickers or fact sheets when you join.

If the membership is too expensive for you on your own, why not ask if your family or your class at school can join instead? Or you could organize a fund raising event to raise money to send to a conservation group.

You can also support organizations like WWF by buying cards, T-shirts, and other products from them. WWF, for example, has a catalog full of wildlife T-shirts and other goods, many of them featuring pandas.

Buying WWF panda merchandise, like this toy, helps WWF fund its panda projects in China.

Could you be a panda expert?

Giant pandas are so rare and well-protected that it is very hard for a normal member of the public to see them in the wild. If you are really interested in pandas, you could become a scientist, a conservationist, or work in a zoo. Then you might end up working with pandas yourself. If you think you might want to do this you should study subjects like biology and chemistry at school.

This adopt-a-panda box is from the WWF. On the front of the box is the name of the particular panda that you have adopted.

Adopt a panda

When you adopt a panda, it does not come to live with you. Instead, you send some money to help care for a panda in a zoo, **reserve,** or **breeding** station. In return, you get a photo of your panda and letters about how he or she is doing. Adopting an **endangered** animal, such as a panda, is a great way to help wildlife and find out more about animals and conservation at the same time.

Where is your nearest panda?

Visiting **captive** pandas is another way to help zoos care for them. You can use the Internet to find out the locations of zoos that have pandas. There might even be a panda at a zoo in your city.

Glossary

adapt alter behavior or structure to cope with changing circumstances, such as the environment or weather or availability of particular types of prey

black market illegal trade that is kept secret from governments and the police

breed mate and reproduce

breeding season time of year when an animal species is ready to reproduce

camouflage markings and patterns that help an animal blend in with its surroundings

captive living in a zoo, cage, or other enclosed space

cell tiny unit of living matter. Different cells help animals and plants to complete different tasks, such as breathing, growth, digestion, and movement.

climate weather conditions and temperature range of a particular part of the world

clone animal created by copying another animal's DNA

coniferous tree that produces seeds in cones

conservation trying to protect nature and wildlife from being destroyed

den place where an animal makes a home or shelter, such as a cave or hollow tree

digest break down food into useful chemicals that the body can use for growth and energy

digit finger, thumb, or toe

DNA (deoxyribonucleic acid) a chemical inside a cell that forms instructions called genes, telling the cell how to work and grow

ecotourism type of tourism that involves visiting a place to see the plants and animals that live there

endangered in serious danger of becoming extinct

extinct no longer in existence

fiber tough, hard-to-digest substance found in plants

fragmentation breaking up something large into small, scattered pieces

gene instruction inside the cells of living things that tells them how to work

gland   organ that releases a particular substance that helps the body work

habitat   surroundings where a particular species lives, such as a forest

isolate   cut off from others

logging   industry that cuts down trees on a large scale, for money

mammal   any warm-blooded animal that feeds its young on milk from its body

mate   when a male and female animal get together to produce young; a partner of the opposite sex

nutrition   food that contains chemicals useful for living and growing

poach   hunt illegally

predator   animal that hunts and eats other animals

pupil   dark hole in the middle of the eye that lets light in

range   overall area where a wildlife species is found

reserve   area of land set aside for wildlife to live in safety

satellite   spacecraft that orbits, or travels around, Earth. Some satellites can collect data about Earth and beam it to computers on the ground.

specialized   specially designed to cope with an unusual habitat or lifestyle

species   scientific name for a particular kind of plant, animal, or other living thing

territory   area of land that an animal lives in and guards for itself

virus   tiny germ. Some types of viruses cause serious diseases.

vitamin   substance present in food that is important for normal growth and nutrition

Conservation groups

Pandas International
Find out how to adopt a giant panda through the Pandas International organization.

P.O.Box 620335
Littleton, CO 80123

World Wildlife Fund (WWF)
International organization that takes action to conserve threatened species, tackle global threats to the environment, and seek sustainable solutions for the benefit of people and nature.

1250 24th Street NW
Washington DC 20037-1175

Books

Bright, Michael. *Bears and Pandas.* New York: Lorenz Books, 2000.

Morgan, Sally. *Mammals.* Chicago: Raintree, 2005.

Penny, Malcolm. *Giant Panda.* Chicago: Raintree, 2000.

Preiss, Byron and Gao Xueyu. *The Secret World of Pandas.* New York: Harry N. Abrams, 1991.

Puay, Lim Cheng. *Vanishing Forests.* Chicago: Raintree, 2004.

Schaller, George B. *The Last Panda.* Chicago: University of Chicago Press, 1994.

Scheff, Duncan. *Giant Pandas.* Chicago: Raintree, 2002.

Solway, Andrew. *Classifying Mammals.* Chicago: Heinemann Library, 2003.

Index